CELEBRATING THE

WONDER

of MOTHER

HOOD

Bobbi McCaughey

with Gregg and Deborah Shaw Lewis

CELEBRATING THE WONDER *of* MOTHERHOOD

Intimate Moments with
My Daughter Mikayla
and the *Septuplets*

THOMAS NELSON PUBLISHERS
Nashville

Published in Nashville, Tennessee, by Thomas Nelson, Inc.

Scripture quotations noted NKJV are from
THE NEW KING JAMES VERSION.
Copyright © 1979, 1980, 1982, Thomas Nelson, Inc., Publishers.

Scripture quotations noted NIV are from the
HOLY BIBLE: NEW INTERNATIONAL VERSION®.
Copyright © 1973, 1978, 1984, by International Bible Society.
Used by permission of Zondervan Publishing House. All rights reserved.

ISBN 0-7852-7048-5

Printed in the United States of America.
1 2 3 4 5 6 — 04 03 02 01 00 99

Photo Credits
Front and back cover: Dana Fineman © 1998 SYGMA

Pages 3, 6, 9, 10, 12, 13, 14, 15, 16, 18, 20, 31, 32, 33, 36, 37, 38, 41, 43, 44, 45, 54, 62, 63, 64, 66, 67, 69, 78, 79, 82, 83, 84, 86, 87, 90, 92, 93, 94, 95, 96, 98, 101, 104, 107, 109, 111, 112, 113, 114, 119, 122: Dana Fineman © 1998 SYGMA

Pages 17, 22, 34, 39, 46, 48, 58, 80, 102: David Peterson/*Des Moines Register* © 1998 SYGMA

Pages 25, 27, 28, 29, 30, 42, 50, 51, 52, 53, 57, 59, 68, 70, 71, 72, 73, 75, 76, 85, 89, 97, 105, 106, 108, 110, 116, 125, 127: Brooks Kraft © 1998 SYGMA

CONTENTS

A CELEBRATION OF THE

WONDER OF MOTHERHOOD

I am the mother of eight children, seven of whom were born on the same day. That doesn't necessarily qualify me to write a book about motherhood. My oldest child has just turned three years old. I don't know yet what it's like to be the mother of a four-year -old. I certainly don't know how to parent teenagers. ❧ But with the birth of our babies, my husband, Kenny, and I embarked on an adventure, given to us by God. He has set us on this course, and He is the One who knows what lies ahead. And since we started, He has showered us with blessings. ❧ One of the ways in which we have been blessed is by the kindness and compassion of strangers. We've sent out more than four thousand thank-you notes to companies and individuals who have shared with us. And we know that thousands more have been praying for us and our family. We have felt the blessing and power of those prayers. ❧ In this book, we will celebrate seven things a mother does for her children. It's my way of sharing with you some of the joys and a little of the wonder that have been Kenny's and mine during our incredible adventure. Thank you for your concern, your interest, and your prayers. May God bless you and your family, as you have been a blessing to ours.

Bobbi and Kenny

(Clockwise from top left)
Kelsey, Nathan, Bobbi, Alexis, Kenny,
Brandon, Natalie, Joel, and Mikayla

GIVES HER CHILDREN LIFE

One of the most wondrous mysteries of the universe is that God gives us, His children, the opportunity to participate in creation. As husband and wife, we can come together in love and create a new human being, flesh of our flesh and bone of our bone. Our children are like us in many ways, yet each baby is a unique creation, a special child of God. ❧ I loved being pregnant with my children, feeling movement and knowing that a wonderful person was growing and developing inside me.

One of the most exciting moments in pregnancy, for me, was when I realized that all those fluttering and other strange sensations I'd been feeling were actually generated by that tiny fragment of life within me. The first movement in both pregnancies felt exactly the same. It took me quite a while to figure it out with Mikayla. But with the seven babies, I knew what was happening right away. They were just little tappings, as if someone were saying, "Hello! Are you out there? I'm in here. And I'm growing bigger every day." What an incredible feeling!

BEFORE I FORMED YOU IN THE WOMB I KNEW YOU,

BEFORE YOU WERE BORN I SET YOU APART. —JEREMIAH 1:5 NIV

God the Creator knows each of my children better than I ever will. He knows their individual needs. He also knows His purpose and will for each one of their lives. For me, as a concerned, loving, and sometimes worried mother, that's an awesome thought. It's the best reason I know to trust Him for my children's futures.

When I was pregnant with Mikayla, as much as I wanted her, I still had doubts. *Do I really want this?* I wondered. I saw other people's kids, especially when they hit that awkward stage when their feet are too big for their body or when half their teeth are missing, or worse yet, in their teen years. And I'd think, *I'm not ready for this!* I had to remind myself, *You are not getting an eight-year-old; you are starting with a baby. You have a few years. And by the time your children get to be teenagers, they may be gangly and awkward but you'll still love them because they are your kids.*

(Left page) Mikayla

I will love You, O Lord, my strength.

The Lord is my rock and my fortress and my deliverer;

My God, my strength, in whom I will trust;

My shield and the horn of my salvation, my stronghold.

—Psalm 18:1–2 nkjv

These verses were especially dear to me during the last portion of my pregnancy. I was at the point where emotionally and physically I felt that I could not go on. But leaning on the strength of God, I was able to make it through one more day, and then another—until November 19, 1997, finally arrived.

Giving birth to a new life is testimony to what a mother will endure for her children. The seemingly endless hours of pain during labor just disappear once that baby is laid in your arms. The entire nine-month ordeal is forgotten as you carefully inspect each hand and each foot, checking for the appropriate number of fingers and toes. Even the months of bed rest required with our seven babies, the weeks in the hospital, the cesarean delivery, seemed a small price to pay for the privilege of giving them life. None of the hardships experienced could diminish the unspeakable joy of finally touching and holding seven living, breathing, and squirming miracles.

(Clockwise from left)
Kenny, Kelsey, Brandon, Nathan,
Alexis, Joel, and Natalie

For You formed my inward parts;

You covered me in my mother's womb.

I will praise You, for I am fearfully and wonderfully made;

Marvelous are Your works. —Psalm 139:13–14 NKJV

Reading this verse, there can be no doubt about whether or not God has a purpose for our lives. Right from the beginning He is fashioning a wonderful work. Each of my children is fearfully and wonderfully made. And our family—the way He has put us all together—is also a marvelous work of God.

We had the babies' first birthday celebration with our families on Sunday, November 8. After church that morning everyone went to Grandpa and Grandma's house where the children napped and the adults ate lunch. When the kids woke up, the party began. Like most one-year-olds, they seemed pretty unaware of what birthdays are all about—except for the cake. They may have eaten some, but they loved smashing it everywhere. ❧ The highlight of the day for me came that evening when we went to church as an extended family. There we celebrated their first year of life with a special service dedicating all seven babies to God—because He gave them to us. They may be ours for a time, but we want them to be His forever.

I KNOW WHAT IT IS TO BE IN NEED, AND I KNOW WHAT IT IS TO HAVE PLENTY. I HAVE LEARNED THE SECRET OF BEING CONTENT IN ANY AND EVERY SITUATION, WHETHER WELL FED OR HUNGRY, WHETHER LIVING IN PLENTY OR IN WANT. I CAN DO EVERYTHING THROUGH HIM WHO GIVES ME STRENGTH. —PHILIPPIANS 4:12–13 NIV

People often ask us, "How do you do it?" Or they say, "I could never deal with seven babies at one time." My confidence lies in knowing that God promises never to ask us to do anything He doesn't enable and equip us for. He blessed us with our children. We can have every confidence that He will provide the strength, the wisdom, and the resources we need to raise them.

READY TO MEET THE DAY

I do it when I smile as I greet my children when they wake up each morning. I do it when I talk to them as I help them dress and fix their morning meal. ❧ What do I do? I set the tone for my children's day. If I am happy and calm, my children are reassured that all is right with their world. If I remind them that I love them and God loves them, they carry that feeling of love and security all day long.

———————————

*O*ne of the greatest stresses of motherhood is the unpredictability of children. But the spontaneity of children also results in some of my greatest joys as a mother. ❧ When I get up in the morning I never know what excitement the day will hold. Is this the day Kelsey is going to stand up? Is this going to be the day Joel finally starts crawling and not just doing the GI Joe squirm across the carpet? It's impossible to anticipate what kids will do or say next. Boredom is *not* part of the job description.

(Clockwise from bottom left)
Alexis, Joel, Natalie, Kenny, Kelsey, Brandon, and Nathan

Our daily morning routine is surprisingly calm. As soon as I hear one of the babies begin to stir, I hurry downstairs to get their bottles ready. Once one baby is awake, the others soon follow. I give them their bottles while they are still in their cribs. While they eat, I dress for the day. ✣ Then I start with the loudest room. Most of the time the babies are just talking, making noises, but sometimes they are crying. Usually Nathan and Kenny are ready first. So I dress them and take them downstairs. By then one of our volunteers has usually arrived, so I have help carrying the babies downstairs. ✣ Joel and Brandon are often second. Once they are dressed and downstairs, I head to Natalie, Alexis, and Kelsey's room. ✣ The family room, which is full of toys and pretty much baby-proofed, serves as Baby Central. There isn't much they can hurt or that can hurt them in the time it takes me to get back upstairs to get the next two. Once everyone's downstairs, I fix Mikayla's breakfast before I sit down and tube-feed Natalie and Alexis. ✺ I realize we'll have to revise this routine as the kids grow and their needs change. Before long they'll be sitting in high chairs eating cereal for breakfast. And after that, it won't be long until they'll go up and down the stairs themselves. ✺ I think once they're eating cereal for breakfast, we may dress them *after* they eat.

Kenny and Kenny

28

Sunday mornings are more hectic. It's just Kenny and me—no volunteer help—and we have a deadline because Sunday school begins at 9:30 A.M. Kenny has always fixed Sunday breakfast for Mikayla and himself. He still does that, then helps get some of the babies dressed. Once everyone is dressed, I sit down to feed Alexis and Natalie. So far, we've been late to church only once.

AND WE KNOW THAT ALL THINGS WORK TOGETHER FOR GOOD TO
THOSE WHO LOVE GOD, TO THOSE WHO ARE THE CALLED ACCORDING TO
HIS PURPOSE. —ROMANS 8:28 NKJV

It is comforting to know that no matter how crazy or how difficult our life may be, God has a plan. I don't have to know the details of the plan. I can rest knowing that God is taking care of the details, and that His plan will only be for our good.

I love watching my children learn new things. I look forward to all those "first" milestones: first teeth, first words, first steps. I like being here to see all that development; I wouldn't want to miss any of those things. ❧ Sometimes people have asked me, "Don't you dread the day they are all walking?" And I think, *No, why would I dread that?* ❧ If they aren't walking soon, that will mean that something might be wrong with them. I'm not pushing them to walk or trying to teach it. But each new milestone makes for an exciting day and another reason to celebrate and be thankful.

People often ask us, "What will you do when you have seven two-year-olds? Seven teenagers?" And we answer honestly, "We really don't know!" It's hard to project what our lives will be like when the babies are older. I can't imagine what it will be like when they are five. I don't even have one five-year-old yet. 🌸 But I do know that each stage has something I am looking forward to. And we have Mikayla to pave the way. That helps a lot. We will have experience with one three-year-old, about two years before we have seven of them.

Mikayla

33

A MOTHER
FEEDS
HER CHILDREN

I loved breast-feeding Mikayla, knowing that I was providing her nourishment, giving her the best food that God had designed for her. While I couldn't nurse all seven babies, I still enjoy feeding them. Because food is such a basic human need, offering nourishment becomes a concrete symbol of love and concern . As a mother, I find fulfillment in providing for my children's basic needs. When I fix them their food, whether I'm warming a dozen baby food jars or mixing formula by the gallon, I am saying to them, "Whatever you are hungry for, whatever you need, I will do my best to provide."

(Left page, left to right)
Nathan, Bobbi, and Mikayla

When we still had babies in the hospital, I would pump breast milk for them. I couldn't nurse all seven babies, but I wanted them to have some of my milk to help their immune systems.

One day as I sat on a couch, using a breast pump, Mikayla climbed up next to me with two bottles in her hands. She pulled up her shirt and positioned the bottles in imitation of the breast pump. She was so proud of herself I didn't tell her that her bottles didn't really have milk in them. We just pretended that she was as successful as Mom.

When they were younger, I made sure that I personally fed every one of the babies at least once a day. With seven babies getting five feedings every twenty-four hours, we needed our volunteer helpers at feeding time. But I wanted to know that each baby had been held and fed by their mother at least once every day. Forty bottles a day usually provided plenty of opportunities to make sure everyone received my undivided attention on a regular basis.

Before they were able to leave the hospital, Natalie and Alexis needed surgery to insert gastrostomy tubes. These enabled us to feed the girls directly through their stomachs, correcting a problem they both had with reflux. As doctors expected, Natalie is already drinking from a cup, along with her other siblings. We anticipate that Alexis won't be far behind. ❧ One night Natalie was lying in my lap while I held her feeding tube and talked to her. I didn't see that her one hand was investigating that thing on her belly. Suddenly she took hold of the tube and yanked. Out came the tube and milk went everywhere. ❧ What a mess!

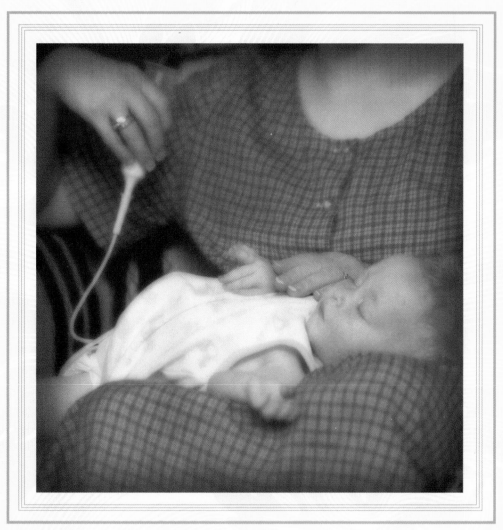

39

While Kenny, Brandon, and Kelsey were crawling around the house on all fours, Joel still belly-crawled, military style. Yet Joel was always among the first to finish his bottle at snack time. Then he would look around, scouting out which of his siblings still had milk left. He'd scoot over and poke or pull that sibling off-balance. When they let go of their bottle, he would grab it, only to have his plans thwarted by Mom, who would return the bottle to its rightful owner. ❧ One day, his cousin Bethany—just one month older than the babies—tried to push Joel off-balance and take his bottle. He let out an indignant howl. That was his trick! He certainly didn't appreciate having it played on him.

Before the babies were a year old, they really got into Cheerios. Our old house didn't have enough room for everyone to sit in high chairs at the same time. So I took the tray off one of the high chairs and filled it with a layer of cereal. Then we put the tray on the floor and placed the babies around it. Instant Cheerio action! You should have seen the arms reaching for the cereal, while their little legs were kicking out behind them. They had fun feeding themselves and trying to feed one another, then rolling over, with hands full of Cheerios. Kenny would climb in and sit in the middle of the tray. We laughed and laughed, and took lots of pictures!

© 1998 SYGMA
Kenny

42

One afternoon when the feeding frenzy on the floor was finished, Kelsey spied a Cheerio that everyone else had missed—hidden on the base of one of the exer-saucers. One of her brothers was in the exer-saucer, but that didn't deter Kelsey. She crawled over, maneuvered herself into the base of the saucer, and got that Cheerio. That's when she ran into trouble. She wanted to sit up to eat it. But, of course, she had no room. She managed to get into something of a sitting position, doubled over under the swinging legs of her brother. Her daddy grabbed his camera and took a picture of her predicament before he helped extricate her.

One day, my brother-in-law Neil saw little Kenny put something in his mouth. "What are you chewing on?" he asked as he began fishing around in Kenny's mouth. After a moment, he pulled out some chewing gum. ❧ We had just given Mikayla and some older cousins a snack and some child had apparently "stored" his gum on the table. Kenny had thoughtfully retrieved it! ❧ We were all totally grossed out. Until ten minutes later, when Neil fished something else out of Kenny's mouth: a big black and orange woolly caterpillar! We decided then that maybe gum, even already-been-chewed gum, wasn't so bad.

As our children grow, we want to have at least one meal together as a family every day. We see other parents whose lives are so busy, they are lucky to have supper as a family once a week. We do not ever want to be that busy. ✄ When I was growing up, my brothers and sisters and I were not allowed to participate in school activities that took too much time away from family. My dad just didn't allow it. We had supper together every night. ✄ Even if it means we have to limit our children's after-school activities, Kenny and I think we need to spend time together as a family every day, just to talk about how the day has gone for each of us.

A MOTHER

COMFORTS
HER CHILDREN

When my children cry, I am the first one they turn to for comfort. So I am the one who needs to know them best in order to figure out what is wrong. Comforting children is one of the greatest responsibilities God gives mothers. But what a privilege that is! Few things in life are more satisfying than wrapping arms of comfort and protection around my little ones and reassuring them that they will be all right.

(Left page, left to right)
Mikayla, Nathan, and Bobbi

As a mother, I feel the most helpless and inadequate when one of my children is hurting. The worst time I remember was when Natalie and Alexis had surgery at three months of age. They weighed only five and six pounds and looked so fragile. ❧ The doctors put them back on ventilators, so when they cried they made no sound. But we could tell by their expressions how much they were hurting. ❧ We weren't allowed to hold them. All we could do was gently touch them, yet it was amazing to see their response to a simple, affectionate touch. Watching the monitors as Kenny or I placed a hand on one of their heads, we could actually see their heart and respiration rates return to normal.

HE WILL FEED HIS FLOCK LIKE A SHEPHERD;

HE WILL GATHER THE LAMBS WITH HIS ARM,

AND CARRY THEM IN HIS BOSOM,

AND GENTLY LEAD THOSE

WHO ARE WITH YOUNG. —ISAIAH 40:11 NKJV

When I struggle to know what's best for my children I find it comforting to know that Jesus is our Shepherd and my children are His lambs. He promises to gather them, *my children*, in His arms and to carry them close to His heart. And since I am a mother—one with young—He promises to lead me gently in the way I should go.

When Mikayla gets a bump or a scrape, she rushes to show me where it hurts, and she looks to me to see if I think it's serious. If I get excited and concerned, her tears turn on and last forever. But if I stay calm and tell her that she is okay, she'll act as if it never happened. ❧ Even when she is really hurt, all it usually takes is a simple hug and a kiss on the affected area, perhaps a Band-Aid, and all is right with the world once more. Neither Florence Nightingale nor Wonder Woman has anything on me; there is incredible healing power in a mother's gentle touch.

(Left to right)
Brandon, Joel, Kenny, Kelsey, and Nathan

One of the questions we are most frequently asked is: "How do you give Mikayla and all seven babies the individual attention children need?" ❦ That is one of the primary challenges we face. And we have to work at it. ❦ Fortunately, only rarely are they all fussy at the same time. Most of the time, seven of the children will be perfectly happy and only one will be out of sorts. That's the one I hold and snuggle and kiss on—whatever I can do that comforts him or her. ❦ So even when we are in a group, I can be alone with one child specifically. I don't have to be separated from the others, or in a different room, to manage one-on-one moments.

We also spend time alone with each child, away from the rest of the family. Each child has gone out to eat with us, alone, in turn. And when I go shopping, I take just one. Not only does that give me a chance to do special things with that one, but it also allows that one child to receive all the oohs and aahs of everyone we meet instead of sharing the attention with a bunch of brothers and sisters.

Our outings have been made possible by a wonderful support network of church, family, and community. I can relax and focus my attention on the one child with me, knowing the rest are in good hands at home.

© 1998 SYGMA
(Clockwise from bottom center)
Brandon, Natalie, Alexis, Kelsey, Bobbi,
Nathan, Joel, and Kenny

54

Brandon is usually our happy-go-lucky boy. He rarely fusses. But one evening when Kenny and I went out he whimpered and cried the entire time we were gone. His grandmother fed and changed him. She held and patted and rocked him. Still he cried. ❧ As we walked back in the door, Val told us, "I'm worried that Brandon's getting sick. He's been crying nonstop." But when she handed him to me he instantly stopped crying and became his cheerful, easygoing self again. ❧ Val laughed and shook her head. "I guess he just wanted his mother." Not even his grandma would do. ❧ As most mothers know, it's almost always nice to be needed.

On the afternoon of June 30, 1998, all the kids and I were in our church's fellowship hall, doing a photo shoot for Simplicity patterns. Pastor Brown came running in to say a tornado warning had just been issued for our area. We whisked up the children and headed for the van. ❧ When I stepped out of the church, it wasn't raining yet, but by the time I ran around the van to open the door, I was soaked. As we drove away after strapping in all the babies and Mikayla, it was raining so hard we could barely see. Trash cans flew across the streets. We actually had to dodge downed power lines. ❧ Since our home had no basement, we went to the pastor's house. There the adults lined up and passed the babies down into the basement—like a bucket brigade. The entire photo crew stayed with us. The basement was packed. The power was out. The excitement and tension upset the babies, so we fed them their bottles, more for comfort than for food, by candlelight. We waited in that basement for an hour before the weather cleared and the sky turned blue again. Then we packed the kids back in the van and headed home, too frazzled to finish the photo session. We had just gotten home, stripped the hot, sweaty outfits off the babies, and changed their diapers, when a neighbor came running over. Another tornado was on the way. This time we didn't bother with the van. Each adult just grabbed babies and ran for the neighbor's basement. The neighbor, our friend Linda Moehring, had three babies in her arms. My sister Michele carried a couple of babies and took

Mikayla with her. Another volunteer helper had the other two. I brought

up the rear with the diaper bags and cried all the way there, thinking, *I*

can't do this again. We sat in another basement for two hours, again

without power. By this time the babies were screaming. So we fed them

by candlelight again. In the first three years we lived in our house,

only once did we have to take refuge in a basement. Then, the first sum-

mer with eight little ones, we had four tornadoes, two on that one day. I

needed comfort before it was over.

(Left to right)
Brandon, Kenny, Kelsey, and Bobbi

Few things warm a mother's heart more than seeing her children comfort one another. Usually it's Mikayla playing the loving big-sister role— consoling a crying sibling or doling out hugs and kisses. ❧ But the babies also show amazing empathy for one another. One day, just after they had been given their morning bottles, Natalie was sitting on the family room floor, when Joel crawled over to her and lay down across her lap to drink his milk. As he nursed, Natalie gently patted Joel's head. ❧ They looked so sweet I could have cried!

The kids don't just comfort one another; they regularly comfort me with their affection. ❧ Joel was the first of the babies to really know how to kiss, and the first to truly give you a hug. He would put his arms around you and draw you close. He would even catch your hair in his hands and pull you as close as he could get you. Then he would lean in, press his lips against your cheek . . . and bite. He didn't realize he was hurting anybody, and he didn't bite hard enough to really hurt. I think he just didn't quite have the hang of what to do with his teeth. His hug and kiss— even with the bite—were full of love.

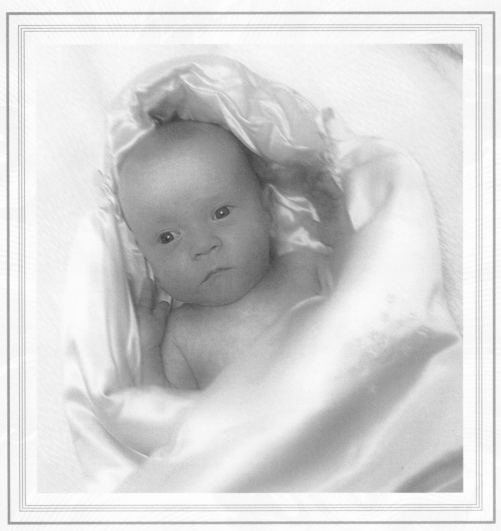

Nathan

As a mother comforts her child, so will I comfort you.

—ISAIAH 66:13 NIV

God the Father knows what it's like to be a mother.

He's a great parenting model when it comes to comforting and caring for

my children. And whenever I'm tired, frustrated, discouraged, or hurt-

ing, He promises to comfort me as well.

TALKS TO
HER CHILDREN

Seeing the smiles on the faces of my children when I talk to them provides some of the most rewarding moments of motherhood. Something about the sound of my voice makes their eyes sparkle. And when I say their names, sometimes they even laugh with joy. ❧ I know how they feel. I remember how I felt when Mikayla first began calling me "Mom." Few moments in life are that precious.

We talked to our babies even before they were born. The last months of my pregnancy with Mikayla, Kenny carried on a regular (if one-sided) conversation with her almost every night. He told her that we were here, her mommy and daddy, that we hoped she was growing okay and that we could hardly wait to see her. ❧ Being in the hospital the last six weeks of my second pregnancy made for a different and much more stressful situation. But Kenny still found time to talk to our seven babies many nights, encouraging them to hang in there and keep growing, speaking our hopes and our love to them even before we could see or hold them. ❧ Then, at birth, the first thing they heard was their daddy's voice greeting them by name.

Natalie

THE SHEEP HEAR HIS VOICE; AND HE CALLS HIS OWN

SHEEP BY NAME AND LEADS THEM OUT . . . HE GOES

BEFORE THEM; AND THE SHEEP FOLLOW HIM, FOR THEY

KNOW HIS VOICE. — JOHN 10:3–4 NKJV

There is genuine comfort in the sound of a familiar voice—the voice of one we know, who also knows us well enough to call us by name. The Good Shepherd knows that, and so should every parent. We not only provide them comfort and confidence, we help establish a strong self-identity when we care enough to speak to (and listen to) our children.

One of the highlights of each day is when Daddy walks in the door at lunchtime or after work in the evening. Each little face turns and lights up with expectancy as Kenny enters the family room and starts his rounds. "Hi, there, Brandon James! Whatcha smiling about?" ❧ "There you are, Natalie Sue. How's Daddy's little girl today?" ❧ All the children follow Kenny with their eyes until they hear their names—not just their first, but also their middle names— Kenneth Robert, Alexis Mae, Kelsey Ann, Nathan Roy, Joel Steven, and Mikayla Marie—and then each smiles or laughs, as if to say, "Yes, Daddy knows me. He said *my* name."

Bobbi with (left to right) Alexis and Joel

I often take one child at a time with me when I go grocery shopping or run other errands; it's a way to give everyone a little individual attention and talk time alone with Mom. But invariably on these fun outings I'll have one or more people see me with one baby and ask, "Where are the others?" 🎀 Tired of giving the obvious answer ("At home"), I've begun saying, "Oh, I left them out in the van." Most people realize I'm only joking and laugh. But I have gotten a few strange looks, and one woman told me she might have to report me to her daughter who worked for social services.

One day before he could even crawl, Joel stopped bouncing up and down in his exer-saucer and began babbling nonsense to the adults in the room. Suddenly all the other babies stopped what they were doing—playing or fussing—to look at their vocal brother. When he finished jabbering, all the others laughed. So a moment or two later, he began chattering away again. The others once more watched Joel intently, and when he finally stopped "talking," they all laughed again. Joel was a stand-up comedian—before he could even stand up.

Kelsey and Bobbi

73

It's not enough just to talk to children, you also have to listen. And that's harder. Sometimes you have to hear what they *aren't* saying. ❧ The day after we moved into our new house, I put the children down for their afternoon nap, as usual. After a while, Mikayla came downstairs.

"Mikayla," I told her, "you've got to go back upstairs and go to sleep."

"I have to go potty!" she told me.

"Then go potty and head back to bed."

Mikayla walked away and I went back to unpacking boxes.

Several minutes later, around the corner came Mikayla again.

"Mikayla, you have to go to bed." This time my voice was more emphatic.

"But I have to go potty."

"Then go potty! And go back to bed!"

Again Mikayla walked away, as if to follow my instructions. Two

minutes later, she was back.

"Mikayla, have you gone potty yet?" I asked.

"I can't find the potty!" she wailed. Poor baby! She'd been wander-

ing all over the new house, looking for the bathroom.

I took her by the hand and showed her where to go.

Bobbi with (left to right) Kelsey, Joel,
Kenny, and Brandon

I believe that reading to her children is some of the most important talking a mother can do. ❧ We have read to Mikayla every day since she was a year old. We started with basic Bible stories in books using simple words. At first we would read before bed at night, but Mikayla loves stories so, we were soon reading throughout the day, whenever she brought us a book and said, "Read!" ❧ Now when Mikayla selects a book, climbs on my lap, and I begin to read, we often have a much larger audience. The babies stop what they are doing and turn toward us to listen. ❧ And I'm enjoying reading those same simple Bible stories with the babies.

Mikayla is at such a fun age right now, and she's such a talkative child that I love having conversations with her. I never know what she will say next! ❧ One day recently I was sitting in the living room when she climbed up in my lap. She put her arms around my neck and looked lovingly into my eyes. ❧ "Mama," she said softly. "Do you know what?" "What is it, Mikayla?" I asked, my heart just melting. "I'm SO sweet!" she answered. ❧ I'm really looking forward to when our seven babies reach this stage. I just don't know how I'm going to stand so much fun and sweetness. I'm particularly looking forward to listening to them all talk to one another. ❧ Imagine the dinnertime conversations we'll enjoy for years.

Alexis

PLAYS WITH HER CHILDREN

Play is a child's work. It's how babies explore and learn about the world around them. For children around the world, play teaches language and social structure. Playing is how babies begin to understand themselves and develop relationships with others. ✿ So child's play is always more than child's play—which means I need to remember that playing with children is important work in my daily life as a mother.

(Left page) Joel

I love tea parties with Mikayla. She usually initiates them. She takes her teapot to the bathroom and fills it with water. She brings it back and pours water into everything—and I do mean everything. Water in the sugar bowl and water in the creamer . . . everything gets water poured into it. Then she goes back to the bathroom for more water. Sometimes she gets cookies or crackers from the kitchen to have at her tea party. But the water is the important thing. And the more the better. ❧ A few times she has tried to have a tea party by herself in her room. She gets in trouble for that! ❧ One time two of our volunteer helpers showed up with a new tea set, a present for Mikayla. They helped her fix hot chocolate for a tea party. They set up the cups and saucers, sugar bowl, and creamer on the coffee table in the living room of our old house. The hot chocolate was in the teapot. They got out some bite-size cookies and placed them in a dish. ❦ Then Mikayla and her friends invited me to "coffee." Mikayla wouldn't call it hot chocolate. She wanted it to be "coffee" and, by golly, it was going to be "coffee"! She kept asking us all if we needed more coffee or cookies. She poured "coffee" and handed out cookies like a real hostess. We ended up with hot chocolate—

and fun—everywhere.

Mikayla and Bobbi

Once a week, Mikayla and I attend a tumbling class. The class is taught by some home-schooled teenagers. The first week, Mikayla cried for twenty-five minutes out of the half hour. But now, every morning Mikayla gets up and asks, "Are we going tumbling today?" She is learning forward rolls, sugar bowls, and bridges. She comes home, pushes the coffee table off to one side of the room, and shows off her newfound skills to me, her dad, and whichever volunteers are here that day.

One night Kenny came home from work with a laser penlight. He tried it out by sitting on the couch and shining it on the top of the coffee table. Little Kenny, who was standing holding on to the edge of the coffee table at the time, grabbed for the light and laughed. Before we knew it, Kenny, Kelsey, Brandon, and Joel—the four who could pull up and stand at that time—had surrounded the table and were grabbing at the dancing light, chasing it around the tabletop and giggling to beat the band.

One morning my mother stopped by before heading out to work. Brandon had just begun to crawl. He crawled over to Nathan, who was just lying there, and took Nathan's pacifier out of his mouth and put it into his own. The pacifier was on a ribbon, still attached to Nathan's clothes. As Brandon crawled away, and the pacifier tugged on Nathan's clothes, Nathan began to whine a little. Brandon stopped. Brandon started crawling, and Nathan whined again, until Grandma Hepworth finally rescued Nathan and gave him back his pacifier.

FOR HE SHALL GIVE HIS ANGELS CHARGE OVER YOU,

TO KEEP YOU IN ALL YOUR WAYS.

— PSALM 91:11 NKJV

It's hard enough keeping one adventuresome toddler out of trouble. With a gang of them going in seven different directions at once, it will be impossible to keep them all corralled. Because of that fact, I like knowing that even when I can't see what may be happening with the kids, there are angels guarding them—angels of protection, forming a hedge about them as they play and explore.

Natalie

89

We were given two four-seater baby strollers. What a wonderful gift they have been for our family! We can take the kids on walks around the neighborhood, over to the park, and even to downtown Carlisle to eat out as a family. One of the places we love to go in the strollers is over to Grandma and Grandpa McCaughey's house. They have a trampoline in their backyard. Grandpa Ken will put Mikayla up on the trampoline and let her jump around, and then Kenny and Ken will put two of the babies at a time up there. Mikayla will jump and the babies will bounce and laugh and giggle.

Once Mikayla has heard a video or tape of a song just a few times, she knows how to sing it. She loves to put on musical variety shows—in which she is the one and only headliner—for her younger siblings. They are an appreciative audience. When Mikayla sings, they usually stop what they are doing and watch her. ❧ One afternoon, Mikayla stood in the living room and performed one of her favorite numbers. At the conclusion, Mikayla gave herself a generous round of applause. Natalie, watching her big sister, copied Mikayla and clapped too! Before long several of the babies knew how to clap and would applaud Mikayla whenever she sang. ❧ A star is born. Or at least a ham.

(Left to right) Natalie and Brandon

One day not long after we moved into our new house, Kenny took a hammer from a drawer in the kitchen to do a small job out on the deck. When he brought it back, he did not completely shut the drawer. ❧ Brandon must have had his eyes on his father. As soon as Kenny walked away from the drawer, Brandon crawled over, reached in and, of all the tools in the drawer, which do you think he grabbed? The hammer, of course. He was going to work, just like Dad. ❧ He wasn't happy when we took the tool away and explained that he'd have to wait a year or two before he could hammer with his daddy.

Most of our babies seem content to stay in the family room of our house. That's where we keep the toys, the swings, and the exer-saucers. But Little Kenny loves to crawl into whatever room his mother is in—especially the kitchen. ❧ I love having him play underneath my feet as I fix supper or mix up the formula for bottles. He has just begun to explore the cabinets. One day he discovered the cupboard with plastic containers in it. As I fixed supper, he pulled those containers out and banged and stacked and played away—within inches of where I was standing. ❧ Having a child choose to be near me—that's one of the sweetest rewards of motherhood.

N ot long after we moved into our new house, Mikayla

discovered the long, straight walkway stretching the length of our

kitchen to the family room. It practically invites a child to run. And

that's what she was doing—just to see how far she could get and how

fast she could get there. She soon attracted an audience. Kenny and

Brandon crawled over and sat near the edge of the room and watched.

They looked at Mikayla, then looked at each other and grinned! You

could almost see what they were thinking, *Hey, that looks like fun! We're*

going to do that soon!

Some of my fun growing-up memories of my own

mother were when she let us play beauty parlor with her as our cus-

tomer. My sister Barb, my brother Pete, and I would brush her hair, rub

lotion on her face and arms, paint her fingernails and toenails, and put

curlers in her hair. Mom just sat there and let us "work our magic."

Sometimes she ended up being quite a masterpiece! She loved it and so

did we. I know moms who would never dream of letting their chil-

dren mess up their hair or experiment with their makeup. But I want to

be the kind of mother my children want to play with.

(Left to right) Brandon and Kelsey

THE IMPORTANT STUFF

When our children grow older they will learn about arithmetic, geography, biology, and history. But what they learn from Kenny and me in the next few years will be more important than anything else they ever learn. At home they will learn how much they are loved—by their parents and by their heavenly Father. They will learn that each of them is a special and unique creation and that God has a plan for their lives. ✲ Within these walls we lay a solid foundation on which our children's character can be built. We pray that our priorities of life, family, and faith will also become theirs.

(Left page, left to right) Joel and Brandon

TRAIN UP A CHILD IN THE WAY HE SHOULD GO, AND WHEN HE IS

OLD HE WILL NOT DEPART FROM IT. — PROVERBS 22:6 NKJV

In the way he should go" means literally, "According to his bent, or temperament." ❧ There are so many things that we as parents must teach our children. Sometimes it is a daunting task. There can be so many questions: How should I do this? When do I teach about that? What's the best way to deal with this child given her unique personality and sensitivities? ❧ I am encouraged knowing that God doesn't intend for us to do it alone. He gives us specific instructions in His Word. If we follow His guidance, He will do the rest.

When I was growing up my dad often told this story from his childhood. His sister cut her leg and was bleeding profusely. Grandma called to Dad and told him to run to get the neighbor. But my dad kept asking, "Why?" Finally Grandma picked up his sister and ran for help herself. By questioning rather than obeying his mother, my dad told us he might have cost his sister her life. One thing Kenny and I want to teach our children is the importance of immediate obedience. When we tell our children to do something, we expect them to do it right then. Only after they have obeyed may they come back and ask "Why?" At that point, we are happy to explain.

Nathan

THIS IS MY COMMANDMENT, THAT YOU LOVE ONE ANOTHER AS I

HAVE LOVED YOU. GREATER LOVE HAS NO ONE THAN THIS, THAN TO

LAY DOWN ONE'S LIFE FOR HIS FRIENDS. —JOHN 15:12–13 NKJV

My mother used to quote this verse to my brothers and sisters and me after we had been fighting. Then she'd make us sit on the couch and hold hands until we decided that a brother or a sister was an all right thing to have. She wanted us to learn to value the other members of our family. I believe family is the best place for children to learn to love and get along with others. And our kids are blessed with plenty of others to practice on.

Many people have worried about Mikayla getting lost in the crowd as the big sister of the world's first surviving septuplets. Those folks obviously don't know our oldest daughter. ❧ Like any three-year-old she needs her share of her mother's attention, and she makes sure she gets her own time and space. ❧ I'll never forget the time she took me by the hand and led me to her bedroom (which had been my sewing room before the babies came home and moved into her old bedroom). ❧ "Mikayla's room!" she announced proudly. "Yes," I told her. "This is your room now." "No babies in Mikayla's room!" she declared. "No, no babies here," I assured her. ❧ And that has become a rule in our house. The babies don't go into Mikayla's room—unless she invites them.

One day, not long after little Kenny started pulling himself to a standing position, he wandered into Mikayla's room and stood up, holding on to the end of her bed. It was the end of nap time and Mikayla was still in bed. She pulled her blanket over her head and then popped her head out. Kenny laughed! So she did it again, playing peekaboo with her brother and laughing with him, until he laughed so hard he lost his balance and went plop! onto his bottom. Mikayla got out of bed, helped Kenny to his feet, and then got back into bed and began the game again.

One day soon after we moved into our new house, two volunteer helpers who did not know each other worked together. As they began to get acquainted, one inquired of the other: "How many little ones do you have?" "Oh!" the second woman responded with a start. "I'm not even married! So I don't have any kids." Mikayla, who'd been playing quietly, looked around the room at her siblings and asked, "Do you want some?"

"HONOR YOUR FATHER AND MOTHER," WHICH IS THE FIRST COMMANDMENT WITH PROMISE: "THAT IT MAY BE WELL WITH YOU AND YOU MAY LIVE LONG ON THE EARTH."

—EPHESIANS 6:2–3 NKJV

This passage is even more important now that I have children. As a child, I didn't always see the value of my parents' teaching. But since the role of parent has passed on, it's amazing how much wisdom my own parents possessed and how I sound just like them. That is how I think of honoring my parents, even though I am now an adult. The things they taught me, the heritage they handed down to me, will be played out in the lives of our children for many years.

As a Christian parent my greatest desire is that my children know Jesus at a young age. We have a responsibility to teach our children about God and to lead them in that direction. ✣ We also want our children to know that they are neither the beginning nor the end. They are but a link in a long heritage of family love and faith handed down from our parents and grandparents, which we hope will live on in their children and grandchildren.

© 1998 SYGMA
(Left to right) Kenny and Natalie

Children always teach their parents a lot. ❧ What are we learning, with one three-year-old and seven babies? On the practical side, we are learning how to be organized, and how to do things faster. Also, Kenny and I have to work together more, as a team, in order to get things done. ❧ Working together means we have to communicate with each other. One of the best things our church has done for us has been to provide us with baby-sitters every Friday night. Each week Kenny and I have time to ourselves—an entire evening when we can talk, catch up with each other, iron out some of the kinks in our schedule . . . and remember why we fell in love to begin with.

TRUST IN THE LORD WITH ALL YOUR HEART AND LEAN NOT
ON YOUR OWN UNDERSTANDING;
IN ALL YOUR WAYS ACKNOWLEDGE HIM,
AND HE WILL MAKE YOUR PATHS STRAIGHT.
— PROVERBS 3:5–6 NIV

This verse talks about one of the most important things I want to teach our children, which is ironic because it's also one of the biggest things my children are teaching me. We've had a lot of things happen the past couple of years that are way beyond our understanding. Our only hope has been to trust the Lord and acknowledge Him. And He has certainly led us down some very interesting and exciting paths.

Another thing we have learned from having seven babies at once is the importance of prayer. When life is going smoothly, when you've got a good job, a happy marriage, and healthy kids, prayer somehow doesn't seem so important. But when something unexpected happens in your life—a life-changing experience like having seven babies—prayer suddenly becomes very real and very important. Kenny and I have learned to pray, and to expect God to answer. We've learned life can be exciting while we wait to see how He answers our prayers.

(Left to right) Brandon and Kenny

BUT WE WERE GENTLE AMONG YOU, JUST AS A NURSING MOTHER CHER-
ISHES HER OWN CHILDREN. SO, AFFECTIONATELY LONGING FOR YOU, WE
WERE WELL PLEASED TO IMPART TO YOU NOT ONLY THE GOSPEL OF GOD,
BUT ALSO OUR OWN LIVES . . . WE EXHORTED, AND COMFORTED, AND
CHARGED EVERY ONE OF YOU, AS A FATHER DOES HIS OWN CHILDREN,
THAT YOU WOULD WALK WORTHY OF GOD WHO CALLS YOU INTO HIS OWN
KINGDOM AND GLORY. — 1 THESSALONIANS 2:7–8, 11–12 NKJV

These verses sum up our job as parents. We are called to
gently cherish our children, to take delight in imparting the gospel to
them, to share our lives with them, to encourage them, to comfort them,
and to instruct them how to live lives worthy of God.

A MOTHER

LOVES HER CHILDREN

All that a mother does for her children—giving them life, feeding, comforting, getting them ready for the day, playing, and teaching—add up to a mother's love. But a mother's love means far more than the sum of her daily actions. ⁂ I find there's a very real spiritual and eternal dimension to it. When a mother feels she is too tired or too overwhelmed to keep on loving, she can call on God's love to help her continue loving her children. ⁂ And to God's love there is no end.

(Left page, left to right) Kelsey and Brandon

When Mikayla was born I loved her with all my heart. It was hard to imagine that I would or could ever love another child the way I loved her. 🙢 Then I had seven more. 🙢 After the babies were born a television interviewer asked how I thought one mother could possibly meet the emotional needs of eight small children. 🙢 I told her that when God created the miracle of love, He gave it an amazing characteristic our human minds can't truly fathom. The love God created, the love He shares with us and wants us to share with others, is infinitely expandable. Love grows to fit the need. 🙢 That's a truth I think you have to be a mother or father to really understand. 🙢

My own mother modeled sacrificial love in many ways. One quick example: With six kids in our family we never had a lot of money. Even if she bought chicken on sale, Mother would seldom prepare more than one for dinner, so there wasn't much meat to go around. When the plate was passed Mom always took the back, so that Dad and her children could have the better pieces. If there were only seven pieces of a cake left, Mom would claim she didn't really want any. She always made sure her family was taken care of before her own needs were met. I noticed that even as a child. And it made me realize that she loved me. May my children see sacrificial love in me.

IF ANY OF YOU LACKS WISDOM, LET HIM ASK OF GOD, WHO
GIVES TO ALL LIBERALLY AND WITHOUT REPROACH,
AND IT WILL BE GIVEN TO HIM. — JAMES 1:5 NKJV

No one else in history has raised septuplets. It would be so easy to feel overwhelmed by the task God has given us. I certainly know that Kenny and I are not wise enough, by ourselves, to do this job well. But all we have to do is ask God for the wisdom required. When we need wisdom to handle seven two-year-olds, He'll provide it. He will even give us the wisdom and love we need for eight teenagers! And He has promised to give us that wisdom generously and without scolding us! Because He first loved us.

(Clockwise from bottom left)
Brandon, Kelsey, Alexis, and Natalie

BUT THOSE WHO HOPE IN THE LORD WILL RENEW THEIR STRENGTH. THEY

WILL SOAR ON WINGS LIKE EAGLES; THEY WILL RUN AND NOT GROW WEARY,

THEY WILL WALK AND NOT BE FAINT. —ISAIAH 40:31 NIV

COME TO ME, ALL YOU WHO ARE WEARY AND BURDENED, AND I WILL GIVE

YOU REST. —MATTHEW 11:28 NIV

Loving and raising my children will require more than wisdom. I've already had enough experience to know I'll need energy and strength. ❧ Whether you have one child or eight, motherhood is a twenty-four-hour-a-day, seven-day-a-week job. Weariness goes with the territory. ❧ But there are also excitement, joy, satisfaction, and immeasurable emotional reward. And on those exhausting days when my supply doesn't quite measure up to their demand, God promises to renew my strength and give me rest.

BEING CONFIDENT OF THIS VERY THING, THAT HE WHO HAS
BEGUN A GOOD WORK IN YOU WILL COMPLETE IT UNTIL THE
DAY OF JESUS CHRIST. —PHILIPPIANS 1:6 NKJV

This verse is reassuring to me as a young mother just starting out on this great parenthood adventure. We have the promise that God won't start something in our lives and then just leave us. He Himself will continue the work until it is complete and perfect. The miracles He began with the birth of our seven babies, He will also continue as our children grow and live out the rest of their lives.

Joel

CONCLUSION

THEN JESUS CALLED A LITTLE CHILD TO HIM . . . AND SAID, ". . . UNLESS

YOU ARE CONVERTED AND BECOME AS LITTLE CHILDREN, YOU WILL BY NO

MEANS ENTER THE KINGDOM OF HEAVEN. THEREFORE WHOEVER HUMBLES

HIMSELF AS THIS LITTLE CHILD IS THE GREATEST IN THE KINGDOM OF

HEAVEN. WHOEVER RECEIVES ONE LITTLE CHILD LIKE THIS IN MY

NAME RECEIVES ME." —MATTHEW 18:2–5 NKJV

One of the reasons I like this verse is because it states that Jesus "called a little child." So many times in the New Testament, Jesus called little children. He must have had children near Him a lot. Obviously, Jesus thought children were important. ❧ Many of the things I do each day may seem mundane to someone else. Changing diapers is never fun; doing all our laundry is never fun. Those things

126

just go with the job. But however humble the work is that I do for my

children, even tasks that others might look down on or despise, God sees

the value of what I do. God counts the sacrifices I make for my children

as loving service to Him.

When I had a job in the workplace, what I did each day may or may not have mattered the next day. Very little mattered the next year. But with children, every single day is important. Even the most tedious and routine things, such as making bottles and changing diapers, have purpose in their lives, to help them know that they are loved and cared for. What I do with my children and the love they learn from me—human and divine—have lasting, eternal value. ✺ I believe a mother's love lasts forever. ✺ Which is why I wouldn't trade the life I have with anyone else in the world.